ROMAN ART

By PATRICIA CORBETT

AVENEL BOOKS

NEW YORK

Roman Art © MCMLXXX by Fabbri Editori, Milan, Italy
All Rights Reserved
Library of Congress
Catalog Card Number: 79-3851
This edition published 1980 by Avenel Books
distributed by Crown Publishers Inc.
by arrangement with Fabbri Editori
Printed in Italy by Fabbri Editori, Milan.
a   b   c   d   e   f   g   h   i

A Roman's proudest boast was his citizenship. During the Roman Republic and well into the Empire, the Roman citizen was a member of a highly privileged minority whose legal rights and prerogatives were manifold and obligations few. The benefits that were the birthright of every civis romanus were rarely taken for granted, as citizenship was not easily acquired but restricted to freeborn citizens of the city of Rome and their direct descendants. To be recognized as a Roman citizen was to enjoy full membership in the most powerful political and military organization the world had ever known.

How did a single city so extend its sphere of influence as to earn the title of caput mundi, capital of the world? What were its origins and how did it develop? The early history of Rome is still a matter of some conjecture. Although legend has it that the city was founded in 753 B.C. by Romulus and his twin brother Remus, archaeologists report that long before that date small farming villages dotted the hills on the east bank of the Tiber. Some time during the eighth century B.C. the inhabitants of these settlements, known as Latins, banded together in self defense to form the Latin League. First conquered by the Sabines, a local tribe, the League then fell to the Etruscans. By the end of the sixth century, B.C., the Latins had regained control of their own territory and founded the Republic. Rome proceeded to establish her claim to Central Italy and then to the entire peninsula (272 B.C.).

For approximately one hundred and fifty years, the Roman Republic – governed by a senate, a body of magistrates and an assembly of the people – directed the full strength of its military power against neighboring peoples and nations, and especially against the North African city of Carthage. The Carthaginians were Rome's bitter rivals in the struggle for control of the main Mediterranean trade routes. The Romans undertook numerous campaigns on land and at sea before succeeding in vanquishing the powerful Phoenician colony (the Punic Wars: 264-241 B.C.; 218-201 B.C.; 148-146 B.C.). Expansion in Greece, Macedonia, Asia Minor, Spain and Southern Gaul (118 B.C.) followed rapidly.

Such significant upheavals abroad could not fail to cause unrest at home. Despite efforts to maintain the peace between a dominant and wealthy patrician class and an ever-increasing number of impoverished and uprooted plebeians, civil war broke out. Ambitious men of war took prompt advantage of the situation: the generals Marius and Sulla vied with one another for political power and recognition, the latter finally attaining dictatorial status. Sulla, the first ruler to undertake a systematic building campaign in Rome, was ultimately toppled by the senate, jealously protecting its prestige and influence (79 B.C.).

Another military leader, Pompey, came to the fore of the political scene after obtaining important victories in Asia Minor. Pompey instituted the first triumvirate (from the Latin words meaning "three men") when he opted to share his power with two fellow generals, Crassus and Julius Caesar. Their union, however, was short-lived: Crassus soon died, and while Caesar was warring against the Gauls, Pompey plotted to undermine his influence in Rome. Determined to foil Pompey's plan, Caesar routed his rival's forces first in Italy, then in Greece. Vanquished, Pompey fled to Egypt, where he was assassinated by the Pharaoh, Ptolemy XIV. Caesar's dictatorship (49 B.C.) lasted barely five years, for in 44 B.C. a group of senators stabbed him to death on the very steps of the senate building.

The Republic continued to be shaken by conflicting interest groups when Octavian, Caesar's adopted son, moved to claim succession. Supported by the Senate, Octavian was challenged by Marc Antony, Caesar's lieutenant. Mustering a private army, Octavian defeated his rival and obtained recognition from the senate.

New threats arose, however, as a coalition of Caesar's old antagonists built up support in the Eastern provinces of the Republic. In a successful bid to crush his new enemies, Octavian formed an alliance with Marc Antony and a third man, Lepidus. The terms of the second triumvirate provided for the division of power between the three rulers: Octavian controlled the Western provinces, Marc Antony governed the Eastern provinces, and Lepidus had command of Africa. Once again the triumvirate proved an unsatisfactory and unstable institution: Lepidus was soon expelled on grounds of conspiracy against Octavian. Marc Antony meanwhile devoted his energies to the reorganization of the Eastern provinces. When it became apparent that many of his political and military decisions favored the interests of the kingdom of Egypt, Octavian acted swiftly, declaring war on the Egyptian queen Cleopatra, Marc Antony's mistress. Octavian's naval victory at Actium in 31 B.C. was decisive. Octavian at this time demanded and received assurance of the loyalty of the senate, which in 27 B.C. granted him the title of Augustus; this date marks the beginning of the Empire, a new era in Roman history.

Augustus instituted a new form of government based on the equal distribution of power between the senate and the princeps, or ruler. He also reformed the army and engaged in a series of campaigns abroad to guarantee the frontiers of the Empire. Egypt's last pockets of resistance were overcome, the Parthians fell beneath the Roman onslaught, the Germanic tribes along the Danube were crushed. The Julio-Claudian line (14-68 A.D.), founded by Augustus, numbered amongst its members some of

3

the most bizarre and debauched figures recorded in all of Western history: Tiberius, who delighted in cruel tortures; Caligula, who made his favorite horse a senator; Nero, who is said to have fiddled while Rome burned.

As Rome and her provinces tottered on the brink of total chaos the army once again provided a savior: Vespasian, chief of the Roman troops in Judea, took strong measures to restore order. The brief dynasty of the Flavians, which continued with Vespasian's two sons, Titus, the destroyer of Jerusalem, and Domitian, was followed by the Antonine Empire (96-192 A.D.). The Antonines restored good government and brought about a period of relative prosperity and peace. Trajan (98-117 A.D.), a native of Italica, Spain, was the first foreign-born Roman emperor; his successor, Hadrian (118-138 A.D.) was also a fellow Italican. Though Hadrian was an able administrator, he was especially renowned for his appreciation of the arts and his generous patronage. The last Antonine, Commodus, was a dangerous madman who reigned for twelve years before he was assassinated by conspirators.

For the next century Rome was governed by her men of war, many of whom, such as Septimius Severus (193-211 A.D.) and his son Caracalla, hailed from the provinces. Anarchy spread through the Empire, with uprisings in Greece, Asia Minor and amongst the Germanic tribes. By the time Diocletian (284-305 A.D.) came to power, the empire was beyond the control of a single ruler. He instituted a tetrarchy, which provided for the equal distribution of power between four men, two "Caesares" and two "Augusti". Diocletian was succeeded by Constantine (306-337 A.D.), who acted to reunite the Empire and founded the city of Constantinople. Constantine is remembered in particular for having halted the persecution of the Christians, as well as for guaranteeing freedom of religion throughout the Roman world. Nonetheless, the general state of affairs continued to deteriorate and by the start of the fifth century A.D. the frontiers of the Empire were no longer inviolable: the repeated and successful assaults by Vandals, Visigoths, and Huns in Spain, Africa, and Gaul heralded Attila's incursion into Lombardy (452 A.D.) and the sack of Rome by Gaiseric in 455. In 476 the last ruler of the Western Empire, Romulus Augustulus, surrendered to the barbarian chief, Odoacre, who was installed as the first king of Italy.

"One of the main characteristics of Roman art is its receptiveness to foreign influence".

*A stretch of the Via Appia near Rome
(Photo by Mairani)*

The history of Rome is not only the record of a city's growth and transformation, but also the story of a civilization that encompassed peoples and cultures on three continents. As the city developed into a conquering nation (its name becoming synonymous first with republican government and later with imperial rule) its culture expanded throughout the civilized and uncivilized world, expressing in no uncertain terms the message of Roman hegemony.

In fact, the story of Roman art is inextricably linked to that of the civilizations it conquered and absorbed: one of the main characteristics of Roman art is its receptiveness to foreign influence. The Romans borrowed freely from the Etruscans and Greeks, as well as from various Oriental cultures, adapting techniques, styles, and structures to the very specific requirements of Roman art. It is recorded that on one occasion, 285 statues in bronze and 230 marble sculptures were paraded through the streets of Rome in a triumphal procession that also included prisoners of war!

However, it was not only through the importation and imitation of foreign works of art that Rome assimilated foreign artistic traditions. Indeed, as the Romans conquered and plundered, they returned with foreign artists as well as with examples of foreign art. It is significant that many of the artists who produced what is known as Roman art were not themselves Roman, but foreign professionals, or even slaves. This extraordinary circumstance may be explained by the fact that painting and sculpture – activities involving manual labor – were considered crafts unworthy of a freeborn Roman citizen. The social status of the artist was no more than of a skilled decorator; he was not honored for his talent and creativity.

While Roman painters, sculptors, and mosaicists have for the most part remained anonymous, the names of a number of important architects have been passed down to us: Rabirius, who designed the Domus Augustana on the Palatine for Domitian (ca. 90-95 A.D.); Apollodorus of Damascus, (early second century A.D.), who laid out Trajan's Forum; and above all, Vitruvius, whose famous ten-volume treatise, *De Architectura*, dedicated to

5

Augustus, was to form the basis of Renaissance architectural theory and practice. The special recognition granted architects points to a fundamental distinction between the roles of the painter and sculptor, and that of the builder. In fact, the architect was held in high esteem for his technical knowledge enabling him to erect those monuments that were the very symbols of Roman power and prestige. Roman architecture was primarily large-scale and institutional, serving the requirements of the state and the convenience of the citizenry. While acknowledging the utility of business and administrative centers, both Republican and Imperial rulers were keenly aware of the tremendous visual impact and propaganda value of lavish, public-oriented building programmes including libraries, baths and theatres. With official patronage, Roman builders originated and developed a number of basic formulas related to institutional design and public construction. Basilicas, amphitheaters, temples, thermae, and triumphal arches were the most characteristic features of the forum, the hub of commercial activity within the city. Domestic architecture also flourished, yet the edification of villas and urban dwellings undoubtedly took second place to the great building enterprises financed by the state and the rulers of Rome.

The enduring achievements of Roman architecture were a product of highly sophisticated construction techniques and skills. The arch represents the key to the most daring feats of engineering accomplished by Roman builders, who first learned its use from the Etruscans. The Romans quickly discovered the usefulness of the arch not only as a decorative motif but as an important structural device. The arch provided a solution to the difficult problem of bridging areas too wide to be spanned by means of the post-and-lintel system. It could also be built up to great heights and was capable of bearing heavy loads. In other words, the arch was particularly suited to large-scale construction projects and often constituted the basic unit in the design of foundations, elevations, and interiors.

The second technical advance introduced by the Romans was a type of cement known as *opus caementicum,* which was formed by mixing lime, clay, and grit, water, and rubble. It was inexpensive, extremely lightweight, and versatile. Poured into wooden molds, the cement hardened to form a sturdy, compact mass, especially useful in vaulting large spaces. *Opus caementicum* was almost always disguised by marble facing or some other sort of surface decoration.

By the second century B.C., the Romans had mastered the basic engineering skills that were to serve them well throughout the periods of the Republic and the Empire, and enabled them to establish at this time the main prototypes for all later Roman architecture.

One of the most familiar examples of Roman monumental architecture was the triumphal arch, erected to commemorate important military campaigns and victories. Originally inspired by the arcuated portals in Etruscan city fortifications, the use of the isolated archway represents a uniquely Roman innovation. The earliest known triumphal arches were not built in marble, but were made of more perishable materials, serving as temporary, decorative structures, or "props," in triumphal processions and pageants. The first stone arches date to the early second century B.C., however, the most outstanding monuments were constructed during the Empire: the Arch of Titus (81 A.D.) is embellished with masterpieces of relief sculpture; the massive triple-arched monument to Constantine is encrusted with bas-reliefs from earlier buildings, as well as contemporary marble carvings.

A purely utilitarian yet aesthetically pleasing design based on the repetition of the unadorned arch may be admired in such feats of Roman engineering as the masonry bridge and the aqueduct, a Roman invention. The Milvian bridge over the Tiber, still extant and very much in use, was constructed in 109 B.C. The system of aqueducts serving Rome was founded at the start of the third century B.C.; the first elevated, or overhead, aqueduct – the Aqua Marcia – dates to the middle of the second century B.C. By the third century A.D., the city was served by a total of eleven aqueducts. The most spectacular of all aqueducts is undoubtedly the Pont du Gard, spanning the river Gard. The Pont du Gard, probably constructed during the early years of the Empire,

supplied the city of Nîmes with approximately one hundred gallons of water per inhabitant daily, transported over a total distance of fifty kilometers.

The arch was used both decoratively and functionally in the theater and arena, two standard Roman building types. The theater was constructed on a semicircular groundplan (Theater of Marcellus, Rome, 11 B.C.); the design of the arena, also known as an amphitheater, resembled that of two theaters joined together to form an elliptical or circular structure with a completely enclosed central stage area (Colosseum, Rome, 72-80 A.D.). Whereas Greek theaters were never free-standing, but conveniently set into a hillside in order to provide the necessary support for the superstructure, the Romans devised a complex system of arcades requiring no external bracing. The articulation of the multi-storied façades of Roman theaters and amphitheaters erected in this manner derives from the alternation of planes and voids determined by the repetition of arcuated openings separated by piers.

One of the most constant and sensitive indicators of architectural taste and evolution is the temple. Early Roman temples derived

7

from Etruscan as well as Greek models and were based upon a plan combining a colonnaded portico with a rectangular enclosed sanctuary, or *cella,* set upon a high platform (Maison Carrée, Nîmes, 20 B.C.; temple of Fortuna Virilis, Rome, second century B.C.). The religious rites, celebrated to propitiate the gods and to honor the state and its rulers, were performed in the open, – in front of, rather than within, the temple. As building techniques became more sophisticated, Roman architects began to prefer cylinder-shaped temples (Temple of Vesta, Rome, first century B.C.). During the Empire, the central plan became increasingly popular, producing one of the most perfect achievements of Roman architecture, the Pantheon, initiated under Augustus and completed by Hadrian in 124 A.D. The Pantheon is formed of a colonnaded portico, surmounted by a pediment, and a large radially panned *cella.* The interior of the temple receives light through a round opening, the *impluvium,* at the center of the domical, coffered ceiling.

Circular structures were not uncommon in other areas of late republican and imperial architecture: funerary monuments and mausoleums were often centrally planned. The mausoleum of Cecilia Metella (Rome, first century B.C.), raised upon a rectangular base, is cylindrical. The arcaded substructure of the tomb of Augustus, once covered by an earthen tumulus planted with cypresses, was built according to a complex radial plan. Erected upon a square platform, Hadrian's mausoleum, now known as Castel Sant'Angelo, represents the most grandiose centrally planned funerary monument of Roman antiquity.

The basilica, the hub of Roman public life, was generally located at the center of the forum. One of the most important building types designed by the Romans, the basilica housed administrative and legal offices, as well as courts of law. Originally derived from Greek temple architecture, the basilica later inspired the builders of the first Christian churches. Although the edifice was constructed on a longitudinal axis, the main entrance was often set into one of the longer sides of the rectangle. The standard basilican plan provided for a nave flanked by two or more aisles, separated by colonnades. Now in ruins, the Basilica Julia, named in honor of Julius Caesar, was once an imposing example of republican architecture: the facade design included two levels of arcades, crowned by a severe attic story. Within, three rows of columns formed two parallel aisles running the entire perimeter of the building. The Basilica of Maxentius, erected at the start of the fourth century A.D., represents the most sophisticated interpretation of the basic basilican model: the use of the barrel vault was introduced in the aisles and the nave was groin-vaulted, resulting in a highly plastic treatment of the interior space.

The thermae were another important category of public building, or building complex. Roman baths were planned on a grand scale and represented self-contained units including hot, warm, and cold baths (caldarium, tepidarium, and frigidarium) and gymnasia, as well as libraries, restaurants, and parks. Such varied attractions made it possible for a Roman of leisure to spend entire days in the baths, exercising mind and body, or simply relaxing in the company of friends. The bathing facilities were segregated by sex; in some instances, however, the women were permitted to use the same facilities as the men, at different times. During the first century A.D., Roman engineers perfected a central heating system that not only served to heat the water for the baths, but allowed hot air to be channeled through conduits built into the walls, floors, and vaulting of the edifice. The Baths of Caracalla (212 – 17 A.D.), now used as a great outdoor theater, were perhaps the most sumptuous thermae ever constructed: the vast domed interior was decorated with mosaics, paintings, multicolored marble facing, and statues in marble and bronze.

Roman dwellings showed great variety in plan. The typical Roman house of the republican era was built around an atrium, or courtyard, which was open to the sky. The family quarters bordered on three sides of the atrium; the tablinium, a large hall-like room reserved for the master of the household, opened onto the fourth side. A small walled garden might be found to the rear of the building. Later developments in domestic architecture betrayed strong Greek influence, particularly evident in the replacement of the atrium by the peristyle, a colonnaded interior court. The apartment house also formed part of the urban

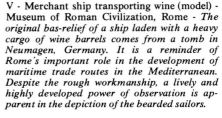

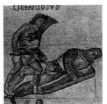

Index of the illustrations

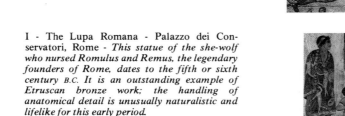

XIII - Scene with actors - National Museum, Naples - *This is another first-century-B.C. mosaic illustrating a theatrical subject. The decorative qualities of the entire composition are enhanced by the representation of traditional theatrical motifs, such as masks and garlands, and by the framing architectural ornament.*
Foreground: Bronze statue of a sitting actor - The Scala Theater Museum, Milan.

XIV - Altar of Domitius Ahenobarbus (detail) - Louvre, Paris - *This marble altar relief, dated to the late second or early first century B.C., illustrates an important public event, the census, together with a sacrificial scene, shown in the detail reproduced here. All the figures are clearly outlined and set in an orderly procession against a blank background.*

XV - Pastoral scene - Roman National Museum, Rome - *This scene evokes an image of primitive Roman society and is part of the relief decoration of a sarchophagus. Romans were always pioud of their pastoral origins and kept exalting them in the art of every period.*

XVI - Tomb of Cecilia Metella - Via Appia, Rome - *The mausoleum built during the first century B.C. for the Roman noblewoman Cecilia Metella stands over ninety feet high and measures approximately ninety feet in diameter.*
XVI - Arch of Drusus, Rome - *It is believed that this arch, situated near the Appian door, was built in honor of Drusus, son of Tiberius, commander-in-chief of the roman legions in Illyria.*

XVII - Temple of Jupiter - Anxur (Terracina) - *Situated on the Appian Way, high above the colony of Anxur, the Temple of Jupiter is believed to have been erected between 100 and 60 B.C. The impressive arcaded substructure and ambulatory of the sanctuary bear witness to the remarkable technical and engineering skills of the Roman builders.*

XVIII - Basilica Julia - Roman Forum, Rome - *As its name clearly indicates, this edifice was erected at Julius Caesar's command, to house the Roman courts and legal offices. Built about 46 B.C. on a rectangular plan measuring approximately 345 by 195 feet, the Basilica rose three stories to a total height of over 115 feet. Within, three parallel colonnades running the entire perimeter of the building formed two arcaded galleries.*

XIX (top) - Theater of Marcellus - Rome - *Caesar is believed to have initiated construction of a theater on this site, although Augustus is responsible for its completion in 11 B.C.*
XIX (bottom) - The Mausoleum of Augustus - Rome - *Augustus intended his mausoleum, built about 27 B.C., to be a monumental landmark in the city of Rome. A conical tumulus of beaten earth was erected over a cylindrical base and an arcaded substructure.*

XX - Examples of military apparel - Museum of Roman Civilization, Rome - *The army of the Roman Republic was a vast, perfectly functioning organization, relying on the support and involvement of all male citizens between the ages of seventeen and sixty. Although, in the early days of the Republic, each soldier was responsible for his own equipment, subsequently provision was made to supply the military at public expense.*

XXI - Standard-bearer - Archeological Museum, Verona - *The standard-bearer of a legion, the largest subdivision of the Roman army, was known as an* aquilifer, *a Latin word meaning "the bearer of the eagle." This relief sculpture, dating to the first century A.D., shows just such an* aquilifer, *grasping in his left hand the eagle-shaped emblem of the Roman legion.*

XXII (top) - Temple of Vesta - Rome - *This small circular temple probably dates to the first half of the first century B.C., when Sulla undertook an ambitious building campaign in Rome.*
XXII (top) - Theater Facade - Aosta - *The principal motif of the theater facade at the ancient site of Augusta Praetoria is that of the Roman arch, the reperition of which creates a rhythmical alternation of voids and planes.*

XXIII - Porta Maggiore - Rome - *An imposing example of Roman city-gate construction, the Porta Maggiore dates to the Claudian era (41-52 A.D.). The motif of the arched portal set into the city walls is Etruscan in origin, but the Corinthian columns, pediments, and mouldings derive from the traditional repertory of classical forms. The gigantic proportions of the inscription accentuate the importance of this access to the city precincts.*

XXIV - Portrait of Pacuvius Proculus and his wife - National Museum, Naples - *This fresco once adorned the Pompeiian villa believed to have belonged to a baker by the name of Pacuvius Proculus. The work probably dates from 60 to 79 A.D. and may well have been executed as a wedding souvenir. This painting of a young couple is one of the most appealing examples of Roman portraiture.*

XXV - Young girl writing - National Museum, Naples - *This delicate portrait of a young girl is one of the most refined achievements of Pompeiian fresco painting. The sensistive rendering of the sitter's thoughtful gaze, the cool silvery tones of the composition, the light brush strokes defining areas of light and shade reveal the hand of one of the foremost artists active between 40 and 50 A.D.*

XXVI-XXVII - Aerial view of the Palatine - Rome - *According to tradition, Romulus designated the Palatine as the center of Rome. In fact, archaeologists have discovered here the remains of primitive structures dating to the eighth century B.C. During the republican era, wealthy citizens built luxurious private residences on the Palatine; the imperial palace of Augustus was also erected on this site.*

XXVIII - The Flavian Arena (Colosseum) - Rome - *The Flavian Arena, also known as the Colosseum, was built between 72 and 80 A.D. by prisoners of war captured in Judea. The dimensions of the amphitheater are overwhelming: the total height of the building is 159 feet. The three arcaded stories of the facade are embellished with Doric, Ionic, and Corinthian columns; the attic level is decorated with Corinthian pilasters.*

XXIX - Entrance to the Colosseum - Rome - *The Colosseum was built to accommodate 45,000 spectators; an efficient system of internal corridors and staircases facilitated access to and exit from the cavea. The Romans were particularly fond of gladiatorial contests and wrestling matches, as well as extravagant, spectacularly staged circus games.*

13

XXX - Commemorative inscription - Civic Museum, Bologna - *The Latin inscription on this rectangular block of Istrian stone commemorates the construction of a building erected during the reign of Trajan (98-117 A.D.), who was hailed as* Divus Caesar, *the god Caesar.*
XXX-XXXI - View of the Colosseum with columns of the Forum Romanum - Rome

XXXII - The Column of Trajan - Forum Romanum, Rome - *This monument commemorates Trajan's victory over the Dacians. Carved out of Parian marble in 113 A.D., the column rises to 125 feet. Trajan's exploits are illustrated in the continuous 656-foot spiral frieze covering the entire surface of the column, which was originally surmounted by a statue of the emperor.*

XXXIII - The Column of Trajan (detail) - Forum Romanum, Rome - *The crudely drawn scenes illustrating Trajan's campaigns in Dacia reveal how little the sculptor is concerned with the lifelike representation of men and objects. The figures are out of proportion, the background sketchy, the composition crowded. The main interest lies in the precise account of historical events. Each episode, rendered in abundant detail, is clearly identifiable.*

XXXIV - Arch of Titus - Forum Romanum, Rome - *Domitian caused this triumphal arch to be erected in 81 A.D. in memory of his brother's victories in Palestine. Built in marble, the arch measures approximately 46 feet in height and 42.5 feet in width.*

XXXV - Bas-relief from the Arch of Titus - Forum Romanum, Rome - *The bas-reliefs adorning the passageway of the Arch of Titus may be numbered among the masterpieces of imperial art. The careful attention to anatomical detail, and above all the illusionistic sense of depth and space, are unique achievements in the history of Roman sculpture.* Foreground: Re-construction of a triumphal chariot.

XXXVI - Hadrian - Museum of Antiquity, Parma - *This bronze bust from Velleia has been identified as a portrait of Emperor Hadrian (117-138 A.D.). The fine modeling of the features is reminiscent of earlier Greek sculpture. Hadrian was a knowledgeable connoisseur and collector who encouraged Roman artists to reproduce and imitate Greek masterpieces.*

XXXVII - Praetorian guard - Louvre, Paris - *This relief sculpture dates to the reign of Hadrian (117-138 A.D.) and represents a group of soldiers belonging to the Praetorian guard. The Praetorians were an elite corps made up only of soldiers from Italy and assigned directly to the emperor.*

XXXVIII - Mausoleum of Hadrian - Rome - *The Mausoleum of Hadrian, constructed between 132 and 139 A.D., was a monumental landmark in ancient Rome. Hadrian's tomb follows in the tradition of earlier cylindrical mausoleums. In the Middle Ages, the mausoleum, known as Castel Sant'Angelo, was transformed into a fortress.*
Foreground: Bust of Hadrian - Roman National Museum, Rome.

XXXIX - Pantheon - Rome - *The Pantheon is considered one of the finest achievements of Roman architecture. Begun by Agrippa in 27 B.C., it was completed under Hadrian in 124 A.D. This temple, dedicated to all the Roman divinities, is constructed on a circular plan. With a diameter of over 140 feet, it rises to a height of 118 feet. The portico has sixteen monumental columns.*

XL - Equestrian monument of Marcus Aurelius - Piazza del Campidoglio, Rome - *The bronze equestrian statue of Marcus Aurelius dates to the period 161 to 180 A.D. Both horse and rider are shown in movement: the emperor appears to be passing his troops in review; his spirited mount seems almost to prance. Particular attention has been paid to surface modeling and anatomical detail.*

XLI - Column of Marcus Aurelius (detail) - Piazza Colonna, Rome - *This monumental column, sculpted between 180 and 193 A.D., commemorates the emperor's successful campaign against the barbarian tribes in Germany. Although the column dedicated to Marcus Aurelius was undoubtedly inspired by Trajan's Column, the representation of events is less prosaic, and expresses a keener sense of drama and a greater tension.*

XLII - Aerial view of Pompeii - *Pompeii, originally built in the sixth century B.C. as a Greek colony, retained many of the typical features of a Greek town, even after it was refounded in 80 B.C. by Roman settlers. Many wealthy Romans erected splendid frescoed villas in Pompeii that were destroyed in 79 A.D., when Vesuvius buried the entire city beneath a river of hot lava.*

XLIII - The Temple of Apollo - Pompeii - *In the detail of the frieze above the entrance, one can see the rhythmical succession of the metope in a perfect state of preservation. In front of the temple is the statue of Apollo.*

XLIV - Villa of the Mysteries (exterior) - Pompeii - *The interior fresco decoration of the Villa of the Mysteries is one of the great masterpieces of antiquity. Although the wall paintings were probably executed during the first half of the first century A.D., the villa itself was built in the third century B.C. and underwent subsequent modifications between 150 and 100 B.C. Further alterations were effected during the first century A.D.*

XLV - The Villa of the Mysteries (fresco decoration) - Pompeii - *This detail demonstrates the illusionistic tendencies popular in the wall painting of the time. Here the artist has imitated architectural forms to such an accurate extent that he has created a trompe l'œil.*

XLVI-XLVII - Villa of the Mysteries (fresco decoration) - Pompeii - *The subject of the frescoes of the Villa of the Mysteries continues to provoke debate and confusion, but it is generally agreed that the scenes represent the enactment of a Dionysian rite of initiation, possibly deriving from an earlier Greek model.*

XLVIII - Villa of the Mysteries (fresco decoration) - Pompeii - *This detail represents another phase in the initiation ritual. Here, a silenus, a companion of Dionysus, holds a wine bowl while a satyr holds a hideous silenus mask above his head.*

XLIX - Villa of the Mysteries (fresco decoration) - Pompeii - *The unidentified winged woman brandishing a scourge forms part of the composition showing the flagellation of a young girl. The gracefully poised figure, with its outstretched wings, is life-sized, measuring approximately five feet in height.*

L - Forum Romanum - Rome - *The Roman Forum, located between the Palatine, the Campidolium, and the Esquiline hills, was the business and administrative center of ancient Rome. During the republican era basilicas, temples, markets, and monuments were erected. Later, under the Empire, construction diminished as building activity in the imperial forums intensified.*

LI - Forum Romanum - Rome - *This view of the Forum includes several major monuments that span the history of ancient Rome: the remains of the Basilica Julia; three columns from the temple of Castor and Pollux, the ruins of the House of the Vestals; and the Arch of Titus.*

LII - Sarcophagus of Acilia - Roman National Museum, Rome - *This tomb, believed to date to the years 260 to 270 A.D., is decorated with figures representing Roman dignitaries or possibly philosophers. The sober arrangement of the forms, the rich folds of the drapery, and the fine characterization of the heads make this a masterwork of late Roman relief sculpture.*

LIII - Sarcophagus - Capitoline Museums, Rome - *In this detail of a funerary work, Roman soldiers are shown dressed for war. The relief is finely modeled, and great attention has been given to the anatomical forms of both the soldiers and the horses.*

LIV - Canopus - Hadrian's Villa, Tivoli - *Hadrian's Villa, built between 118 and 138 A.D., constitutes one of the earliest full-scale attempts at landscape architecture. Replicas of famous Greek and Oriental monuments adorn the grounds. The Canopus reproduces in miniature the Egyptian temple of Serapis in Alexandria.*

LV - Maritime Theater - Hadrian's Villa, Tivoli - *The Maritime Theater, also known as the Nympheum, consists of a circular pool measuring over 130 feet in diameter, surrounded by an Ionic colonnade. Hadrian's island of retreat was situated at the center of the Maritime Theater.*
Foreground: Marble frog from the remains of a fountain - Civic Museum, Bologna.

LVI - Gladiators and wild beasts - Villa Borghese - Rome - *This third-century-A.D. mosaic, discovered at Terranuova, illustrates a perennially popular Roman spectator sport, lightly armed gladiators pitted against wild beasts. There is little sense of depth in this composition, and the figures are crudely drawn, but the dramatic event is vividly expressed.*

LVII (top) - Arch of Septimius Severus - Forum Romanum, Rome - *This three-bayed triumphal arch, built in 203 A.D. in honor of Septimius Severus and his two sons, measures seventy-five feet in height and eighty-two feet in width.*
LVII (bottom) - Arena - Verona - *The oval amphitheater of Verona was constructed during the first century A.D. While only four bays of the three-storied facade are preserved, the two levels of internal arcades have survived intact.*

LVIII - Mattei Sarcophagus - Capitoline Museums, Rome - *This third-century-A.D. sarcophagus relief represents the god Mars and the Vestal Virgin Rhea Silva, whose offspring were the twin founders of Rome, Romulus and Remus. The composition of the scene is crowded and somewhat confused, only the figures of the legendary protagonists being immediately identifiable, due to their large dimensions and prominent position in the foreground.*

LIX - Ludovisi Sarcophagus - Roman National Museum, Rome - *The Ludovisi Sarcophagus dates to the middle of the third century A.D. The battle scenes show Roman soldiers struggling with barbarian warriors. The entire composition is an intricate mass of tangled bodies, armor, and horses, forming a rich yet uniform pattern of light and shade.*

LX - Arch of Constantine - Rome - *This massive triumphal arch, was erected during the years 312 to 315 A.D. in honor of Constantine, Rome's first Christian emperor. The ornate three-bayed facades of the arch bear numerous relief sculptures removed from earlier imperial monuments, as well as contemporary works that illustrate Constantine's military exploits.* Foreground: Statue of Constantine - Milan.

LXI - Basilica of Maxentius - Forum Romanum, Rome - *This basilica, initiated by Maxentius in 306 A.D., was completed by his brother Constantine in 312 A.D. The design of the edifice was based on a central groin-vaulted nave, flanked on either side by three barrel-vaulted bays forming lateral aisles. The interior was illuminated by a row of arched windows, as well as by a series of broad semicircular openings above the central nave.*

LXII - Portrait of a woman - Louvre, Paris - *Originally in Fagyum in Egypt, this painting demonstrates the exceptional realism and sensitivity of some aspects of Roman art.*

LXIII (top) - Pont du Gard - Nîmes - *A masterpiece of civil engineering, Pont du Gard was actually built as an aqueduct in the late first century B.C. The three stories of arcades span a total of 902 feet. The water flowed through covered conduits built into the top level.*
LXIII (bottom) - Theater of Gerasa - Gerasa (Jerash) - *The complexity of detail in this structure illustrates the extent of the development of architecture in the Roman colonies.*

15

The 'Lupa Romana'

I

Dancing girls

Dancer

Ship being loaded with wheat

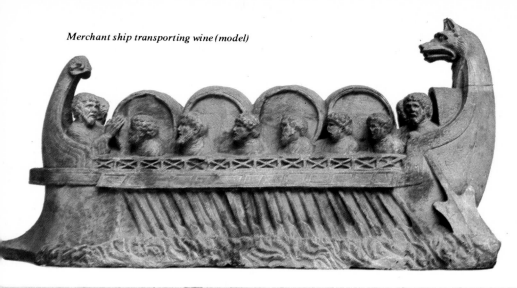

Merchant ship transporting wine (model)

Servers at a banquet (model)

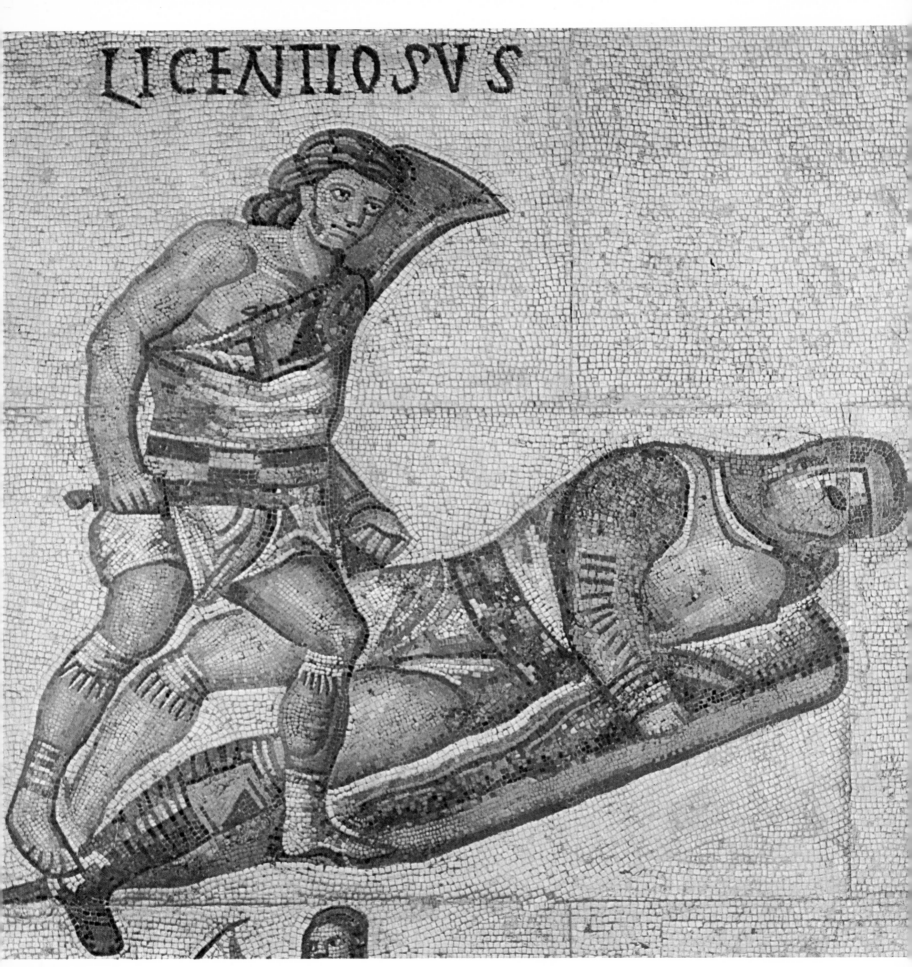

LICENTIOSVS

Two gladiators   *Man wearing a cape*

IX

Banquet scene

X

Augustus Pontifex Maximus

Temple of Ancyra

XI

Comedy scene with actors

Scene with actors

Sitting actor

XIII

Altar of Domitius Ahenobarbus

Tomb of Cecilia Metella - Rome, Via Appia

Arc of Drusus

XVI

XVII

'Basilica Julia' - Rome, Roman Forum

Theatre of Marcellus - Rome

The Mausoleum of Augustus - Rome

XIX

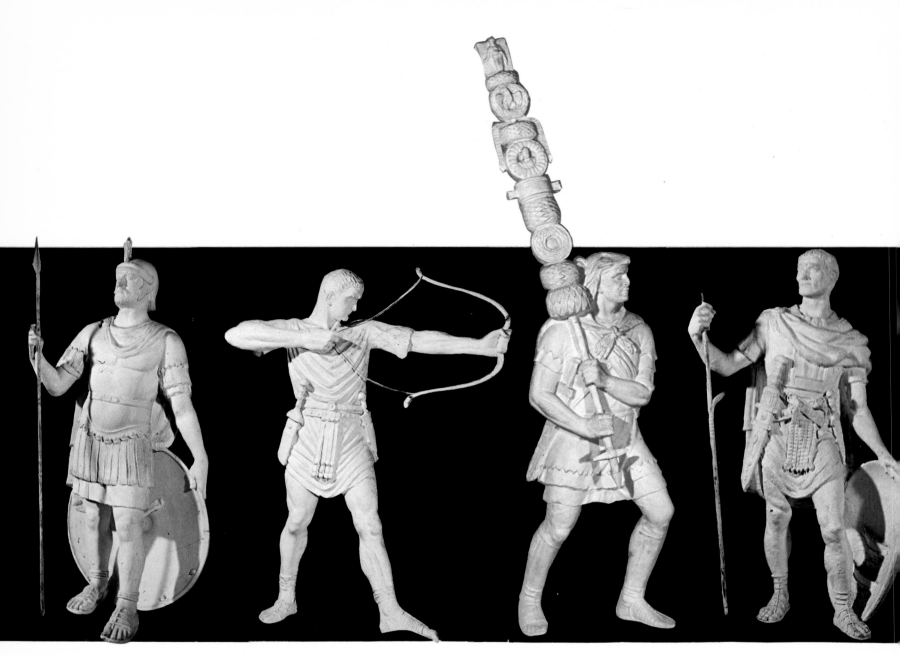

Examples of military apparel

Temple of Vesta - Rome

Theatre façade - Aosta

XXII

Porta Maggiore - Rome

Portrait of Pacuvius Proculus and his wife

Young girl writing

Aerial view of the Palatine - Rome

The Flavian Arena (Colosseum) - Rome

View of the Colosseum with Columns of the Forum Romanum

The Column of Trajan - Rome, Forum Romanum

The Column of Trajan (detail)

Arch of Titus - Rome, Forum Romanum

Bas-relief from the Arch of Titus

Hadrian

Pretorian guard

Mausoleum of Hadrian - Rome

Portrait of Hadrian

Pantheon - Rome

Equestrian monument to Marcus Aurelius - Rome, Piazza del Campidoglio

Column of Marcus Aurelius - Rome, Piazza Colonna

Villa dei Misteri (exterior) - Pompeii

Villa dei Misteri (fresco decoration) - Pompeii

Villa dei Misteri (fresco decoration) - Pompeii

Forum Romanum

L

Sarcophagus of Acilia

Sarcofagus

Maritime Theatre - Tivoli, Hadrian's Villa

Fog of marble

LV

Gladiators and wild beasts

*Arch of Septimius Severus -
Rome, Forum Romanum*

Arena - Verona

Mattei Sarcophagus

LVIII

Ludovisi Sarcophagus

Arch of Constantine - Rome

Basilica of Maxentius - Rome, Forum Romanum

Constantine

Portrait of a woman

LXII

Theater of Gerasa (Giordania)

Illustrations from the Picture Archives of Fabbri Editori, Milan
Printed in January 1980, at the graphic plant of Fabbri Editori - Milan, Italy